Father of the Groom
How To Give A Killer Wedding Speech
Tools, Tips, and Tricks to be a Great Wedding Speaker

By The Wedding Mentor

Table of Contents

About Story Ninjas

THE PROBLEM WITH BEING FATHER OF THE GROOM

If you're reading this book, there's a good chance you've been chosen to be the Father of the Groom for a wedding.

Congratulations!

You just just got suckered into doing a ton of work...

Seriously though, it goes without saying that the Father of the Groom has one of the most difficult jobs in the entire wedding party. Aside from the officiant, and perhaps the best man, the Father of the Groom duties are by far the most numerous and diverse. From holding rings and coordinating with catering personnel, to handling last minute "fires", and mingling with guests, the title of Father of the Groom carries with it a long list of responsibilities.

Chief among them is your Father of the Groom speech.

For anyone who's attended weddings before, you've probably seen the good, the bad, and the ugly. Some speakers give great speeches that energize the crowd and leave a memory that will last a lifetime. While others fumble through notes and put the audience to sleep. Worst of all is when a speaker fails so epically, that they leave people feeling awkward or uncomfortable. Intentional or not, this can have a long lasting effect that taints the entire day for years to come. Whether it's broken microphones, drunken stumbling, or lack of preparation, there are a million things that can go wrong during the Father of the Groom speech.

The purpose of this book is to help you navigate through the common pitfalls most fathers of the groom make, and help you give a killer Father of the Groom speech. In this book, I'll teach you how to prepare, brainstorm, outline, rehearse, and execute your speech. We'll discuss all of the duties of the Father of the Groom so you're completely prepared for the day of the wedding. This will include coordinating with the groom and bride, dress and appearance, interacting with friends and family, recording the speech, alcohol consumption and so much more. Additionally you'll learn the most common issues that happen during the Father of the Groom speech and how to overcome them. Moreover I provide an example speech at the end of the book, that can be tweaked for your particular needs.

Ultimately, this book will provide fathers of the groom with the tools, tips, tricks--and most importantly the confidence--they'll need to give a killer speech. By the end of the event, you'll walk out feeling like a hero and knowing you gave it 110%.

WEDDING MENTOR

So what gives me the authority to teach you how to give the Father of the Groom speech?

You maybe wondering why I feel as though I am qualified to write a book about Father of the Groom speeches. Well I'm glad you asked. I've been lucky enough to give multiple wedding speeches in front of crowds ranging between 100 to 500+ guests. I have also officiated weddings, given toasts at engagement parties, and helped others prepare wedding speeches. Aside from that I have served as a public speaker in many capacities. In the military I gave multiple briefings to high-level officials and groups of hundreds. I've also served as a ToastMaster for several years. I've spoken in several school volunteer events, and in my free time I maintain a YouTube channel the teaches people how to reach their full potential. While I do not consider myself a guru, I do believe I my experience will help others give the best speech that they can possibly give.

I'm not writing this book because I think I know more than the experts. Rather, I decided to write this book because this is the one I would have wanted each time I was preparing for my Father of the Groom speeches.

A step-by-step guide.

This will help you prepare and execute the Father of the Groom speech all the way through.

Luckily, you won't have to guess through the process like I did. In this book you'll learn specific steps and action items that will make the process clear and simple. This walkthrough will help you build the confidence needed for the day of the wedding. That way you can give the best speech you possibly can. I'll teach you each phase of the speech process. You'll learn how to prepare, brainstorm, outline, rehearse and execute the speech. I'll provide you with an example script, including body language suggestions. Moreover, I'll list all of the duties of the Father of the Groom and prepare you for all of the pitfalls most fathers of the groom make during the wedding. I not only discuss how to prepare the speech but I also tell you exactly what to expect when you're up there on stage. I'll give you practical advice that explains what to do before, during and after the speech. We'll discuss common mistakes and pitfalls to look out for.

Ultimately, you'll devise a speech that will not only commemorate the couple's special day, but leave you looking like a hero in the eyes of everyone at the event.

CONGRATULATIONS! (for real this time)

If you bought this book that means you probably have been asked to be the Father of the Groom at your friend or family member's wedding. Or, perhaps you're the groom or bride and you want to give this book to your Father of the Groom. Whatever the case may be, congratulations! Weddings might possibly be the most important day of a person's life, and the Father of the Groom's speech is by far the most important speech of the day. That's right, I said it. More than the officiant's speech, and the couple's vows, the Father of the Groom is the one speaker who represents everyone in the ceremony. If done correctly, the speech will set a precedent for the day, the marriage, and the years to come.

WHO NORMALLY SERVES AS Father of the Groom?

Not always, but more often than not, the Father of the Groom is chosen because he is the father of the groom. However, sometimes uncles, or men who served as foster parents, guardians, or mentors of the groom (or sometimes of the bride). Occasionally, it is a mutual friend that the couple believes is best suited to represent them. In any case, this role brings with it quite a few responsibilities and obligations. Just a few of the standard obligations are renting a tuxedo, or buying a suit (more on this later); purchasing plane tickets; holding rings and wedding vows; acting as a liaison between family members, and, of course, giving the Father of the Groom's speech. Many guys fear being selected as Father of the Groom simply because of the numerous duties that are associated with the role, not to mention having to face the greatest fear most people have--public speaking. And their fear is justified. If handled incorrectly, this speech can not only cause awkwardness for everyone involved, but in some instances, can actually ruin the mood of the festivities. Just imagine the Father of the Groom puking all over the groom and bride because of a mixture of nerves and alcohol. (Pro tip: Don't drink alcohol before your speech. More on this later.)

The purpose of this book is to help you come up with a killer speech that will leave the crowd wanting more, and the groom and bride elated with their decision to choose you to represent them on their most special day. Since choosing you was essentially the first major decision they've made as a married couple, your speech will go a long way in helping to set the tone for their marriage.

ROLE OF THE Father of the Groom

Some might say that the Father of the Groom actually has the most difficult job in the entire wedding party. His responsibilities include, but are not limited to, the following:

- helping the groom and bride prepare for the wedding
- transporting things to the event
- Coordinating with staff
- Interacting with guests
- leading the wedding party
- Assisting with last minute issues that arise
- preparing and delivering a speech in front of an audience
- Keeping the groom and bride calm
- holding the rings
- holding the wedding vows

As you can see, there are several responsibilities that the Father of the Groom performs during the course of the wedding. But by far the most important duty is to prepare and deliver a speech that will frame the event and create a context for the day. When done correctly, this speech can be the culmination of all of the days, months, and years leading up to the day's events and be remembered by all as the capstone of the couple's relationship.

Therefore, we will cover the main areas that will prepare you to perform the duties of the Father of the Groom like a pro. First is overall preparation. Second is the brainstorming the speech. Next is outlining. After that is rehearsal. And last is execution of the speech.

PREPARATION

Time frame: As soon as possible, but no later than one month before the wedding day

Once the groom and bride have asked you to perform the duties of the Father of the Groom, and you've accepted the responsibility, the first thing you want to do is schedule a time to speak with them. This can be a meeting at a coffee shop, or a phone call after work. How you work it will really just depend on availability and how far away you live from the couple. In any event, you should ask them the questions below (at a minimum), which will help you develop your speech and understand your audience:

- How long do I have to give this speech?
- ☐ Most speeches are 5 to 10 minutes. Anything longer than that is not recommended, even if allotted more time.
- Where will the speech be held?
- ☐ For example, is it at the same venue that the wedding ceremony took place? Is it at a different place, like a reception hall? Or is it outside? The Father of the Groom needs to factor in weather conditions.
- Who is my audience?
- ☐ Most of the time this will be family and friends. Occasionally the groom and bride will invite office colleagues and business partners. Depending on how formal they want their speech, or how religious the crowd is, this will dictate some of your speech decisions. The main thing you need to decide is

whether or not to give a PG, PG-13, or rated R version.

- What is the theme of the wedding?
- ☐ This may end up being a theme for your speech.
- Is anything off limits?
- ☐ Do they want it to be highbrow or lowbrow? Are curse words acceptable? Are jokes acceptable, or do they want it to be straightforward and serious? Are they looking for something heartfelt, or are they looking for something funny? Are there any topics that are off-limits or too sensitive that you should avoid?
- Will there be alcohol?
- ☐ The answer to this is important so that you know in advance and have a game plan for how to deal with alcoholic beverages before you speak (read on for details).
- When will the speech be given?
- ☐ Right after the ceremony? Or, while everyone eats? Or, will the speech be given later in the reception, perhaps before dancing?

Gathering this information is paramount to your success because it will: 1) set the groom and bride at ease (because they will see that you have their best interests in mind), and 2) provide valuable insight into the environment where you will be speaking, and the audience that you will be speaking to. Also, if you get a chance, you may want to discuss these details with the maid (or matron) of honor or best man. This will allow you to deconflict efforts so that you both don't end up telling the same stories during your speeches. Lastly, you may want to separate the groom and bride and ask them specific questions. For example, you may want to ask both of them individually about the day they met, and get two different perspectives. If they give wildly different answers, this can sometimes lead into a really good joke or funny story. You could also ask them what they think is the best quality in their partner; and the quirkiest; and if you're really risky, the worst quality!

BRAINSTORMING

Time Frame: No later than three weeks before the wedding

Brainstorm for your speech. This is a free flow brainstorming session, where you will write down anything that comes to your mind. Below are a few ideas to get the juices flowing. In most cases you should focus on the bride because the Father of the Groom normally talks about the groom. However, some weddings do not have the Father of the Groom, and in some situations the Father of the Groom may be a relative or friend of the groom, in which case it would be appropriate to talk about the groom.

1. How do you know the bride?
2. How did you meet the bride (or the groom)?
3. Are there any funny stories you have about the bride or groom?
4. Heartwarming stories about the groom or bride?
5. Best qualities of the groom or bride?
6. Funny stories about the groom or bride?
7. What do you think about the marriage?
8. Which theme do you think would be most appropriate? For example, a science fiction or Star Wars theme for geeky couples, or an athletic theme for sports enthusiasts.

OUTLINING

Time frame: No later than two weeks from the wedding

Right around two weeks out--if you haven't done so already--you need to start outlining. This will give you time to flesh out the speech, make corrections, and get in some practice before the wedding. At a minimum, you should make an outline with the following points:

1. **Introduction:**
   i. Hello, my name is...
2. **Joke:**
   i. To lighten the mood.
3. **Question:**
   i. To engage the crowd (normally thought-provoking).
4. **Theme:**
   i. Set the tone of your speech.
5. **Credibility:**
   i. Explain how you know the bride.
6. **Funny/Heartfelt Story:**
   i. Story about the bride, possibly alluding to a quirky flaw or admirable quality.
7. **Hope:**
   i. What is your one hope for the bride?
8. **Transition to the groom:**
   i. Explain how you know the groom.
9. **The groom's perspective:**
   i. What the groom says about the bride.
   ii. Or, if you know the groom well, what is she like
10. **Give thanks:**

i. Explain how thankful you are that the groom came into the bride's life, because she helped the bride achieve the hope you had for him.

For an example script, refer to the example section later in this book.

REHEARSAL

Time frame: no later than one week before the wedding

Rehearse this speech as many times as possible. Every speech I've given has been rehearsed multiple times before going in front of an audience. If there is one thing I've learned, the more you rehearse, the better the speech turns out. If you can get to a point where the content and words in your speech are no longer difficult for you to remember, you can then add flourishes to your speech. These include hand gestures and advanced body language, clever jokes, and interactions with the crowd/props. These only work when you're not focusing on the words of the speech. Simply put, you can't do anything advanced before mastering the basics.

Day 1

Day 1 is the baseline. Practice the first section of your speech at least three or four times, only focusing on the beginning section of the speech. Once this is done, practice three or four times with the beginning and middle of the speech. Lastly, practice three or four times with the beginning, the middle, and the end of the speech--including the toast. Total, you should do a *minimum* of nine practice runs. I personally recommend 12 to 15.

Day 2

Record yourself giving the full speech. Do this five times at a minimum. After each recording, take another look at the speech. Pay attention to how you sound and make corrections as necessary. Pitch and intonation can greatly affect the delivery of your speech. Try to avoid a monotone voice, stuttering, and filler words such as "um," "ah," "like," and "you know." Attempt to add pauses to areas you want to place emphasis on.

Day 3

You'll need the recorder again, but this time you'll use a timer as well. Keep the speech within the time frame you've been given. If no guidance was given, assume you will be allowed five to ten minutes tops. This is normally the "sweet spot" of an audience's attention span, although seven minutes is really the golden zone.

You may think that if you're giving a really great speech, you can talk longer than ten minutes. While that may be true for some unicorns, the reality is: you're probably not that good of a speaker. If you blither on, you risk losing the audience completely. In the words of world famous speaker, Les Brown, "The greatest speakers make the fewest words go farthest."

Better to leave them wanting more, than wishing you would shut up.

Day 4

Use a mirror or video camera to watch your movements. Believe it or not, body language actually makes up over 90% of communigroomion. Even if you have the best organization, structure, and verbal delivery, if your body language is not congruent, you could still ruin the speech. That's why this is so important for you to practice your movements. Depending on the size of the audience, you may need to pace around the speaking area--especially if you don't have a microphone. In this case, you should practice projecting your voice and moving from one area to another. A general rule of thumb is to move after each main point in your speech. For example, if you start on the left hand side of the room, describe how you met the bride. Then move to the middle of the room where you can talk about the groom. At the end of the speech, go toward the right side of the room, and give the toast. Thankfully, most weddings will have a microphone. Practicing while holding a prop (like a hairbrush) will allow you to get accustomed to handling a microphone. Additionally, you should refrain from using flamboyant body movements--unless they're part of the story--as they can distract the audience from the content of your speech.

Day 5

If you can, practice the speech in front of another person that is not the groom or bride. This person should preferably be someone who is not going to attend the wedding so that you don't ruin this speech for them. However, in some cases this is not possible. If you have a spouse, ask them to listen to the speech and give you feedback. Try to choose someone who will give you good, honest, and constructive criticism. The last thing you want is a sugar-coated review. Although it's nice to know what the speech's strengths are, the main thing you need to know are the weaknesses. While it may not be a pleasant experience, it's far better to find out that your speech sucks from one person, rather than from a crowd of hundreds of people the day of the wedding. From their feedback, adjust accordingly. If a joke's not funny, remove or replace it. If a story seems too long, or to short change it.

If you can't find someone to listen to you, then you'll need to record yourself with a camera. Judging yourself can be the hardest thing to do, which is why I recommend a friend. But if you have no other choice, you're going to have to be completely honest with yourself. When you review the speech pretend your other people in the audience. A parent, a sibling, a coworker, a friend. Does the speech still make sense? Is it appropriate? Are there places you can add or subtract from?

Day 6 (and the rest of the time leading up to the wedding day)

The more you practice, the better you'll become. You won't stutter over your words. You're body language will be congruent. And you can add flourishes to the speech. Also, as you rehearse the speech, it may evolve into something even better. This is the normal course for all forms of communigroomion. Feel free to make minor corrections up until the day before the wedding. From there on out, you should keep the content the same. Tiny word changes (from happy to glad) are fine, but major rewrites in the content can lead to disaster.

Using Note Cards (Or Notes Written on Paper)

A word of caution against notes and cards: I personally don't think they're a good idea. First and foremost, notes make the speech feel insincere. Reading from notes is distracting for the audience, and it screams "lack of preparation." It tells the groom and bride that you do not consider their special day important enough to practice for it. Furthermore, it conveys an amateurish vibe, which not only reflects poorly on you, but also on the groom and bride, and their respective families. Remember, the best man and maid/matron of honor are the two people who represent the couple. The last thing anyone wants, is to see you rambling on for 15 minutes about the first time you went cow-tipping in the tenth grade. Worse yet, no one wants a speaker whose nose is buried in notecards during the entire speech. Notice that the title of this book is "How to Give a Killer Father of the Groom Speech," not

"How to Read Your Father of the Groom Speech from Note Cards and Bore the Audience to Death." If you're still not convinced, I've written a list of issues that can arise from notecard use:

- You could forget the note cards.
- You could lose them.
- Your kids or someone else could mess them up or mix them up.
- In most cases, you'll be holding a microphone. Trying to shuffle notes while holding the mic is not an easy task-- especially with the pressure of speaking in front of a large group of people.
- Nerves are easy to detect if a shaky hand is holding the cards. It's much harder to spot if your hand is in your pocket.
- Moreover, if you're extra nervous, you run the risk of dropping the cards--which becomes extremely problematic.
- You could lose your place while reading, because you don't remember what you wrote, you don't understand what you wrote, or you can't read what you wrote. I've seen all of these happen in multiple speeches. No matter what, freezing up during the speech is never a good thing.

Now that I've beaten that horse to death, let's move on to the execution phase.

EXECUTION

Timeframe: The Day of the Wedding

On the day of the wedding the Father of the Groom *must* be prepared. There will be little time to practice the speech, and there will be several expected (and unexpected) duties that you'll be required to perform throughout the day. As the Father of the Groom, you not only have to prepare yourself (getting dressed, driving to the venue, herding children, etc..) but also find time to rehearse if you can. Practice early because it is likely that you'll be called upon to help with the following tasks:

- Finding the groom/bride
- Finding family members
- Helping bridesmen with tuxes
- Leading bridesmen in the wedding ceremony
- Keeping the groom/bride from freaking out
- Keeping family members from freaking out
- Instructing staff
- Taking pictures
- Speaking with family and friends
- Escorting bridesmaids
- Last minute problems/changes
- No-shows
- No microphone or finding a microphone
- Bad microphone
- Coordinating with camera people
- Food preparation
- Meeting friends and relatives

And the list goes on and on...

Despite the never ending amount of things you'll have to take care of, there will be pockets of time when you can rehearse. I highly recommend that you take advantage of those moments to go over your speech--even if it's just in your head. While you're getting ready you'll have a few key moments to practice. Rehearse your lines in the shower, or afterward, while you're changing. If you have to iron your shirt, that's another perfect opportunity to review your speech. As I mentioned before, the more you practice, the better you feel and the better you get. This will keep the key points fresh in your mind throughout the day.

Alcohol

I'm going to pause here to address a very important topic... Alcoholic beverages.

If you're like me, you probably enjoy a drink every now and then. This is especially true at events like weddings, where the bar is open. However, take it from me, drinking before your speech can spell disaster. If you accidentally drink too much, and get snookered before the speech, you may end up ruining all of your hard work. Just imagine all of those weeks you spent brainstorming, outlining, and rehearsing your speech, only to ruin it because you got too drunk to give the speech. Although a tipsy speaker can get a few laughs initially, most audiences grow tired of a drunken speech as time goes on. My recommendation is to hold off on drinking any alcoholic beverages until after you have given your speech. Consider it a well-deserved reward.

After the Wedding Vows/Nuptials

After the ceremony, try to mingle with as many people as you can. Start with people you know, then move on to people you don't know. Topics of conversation could be:

- Parts of the ceremony that they liked
- How they know the groom or bride
- If they're your friends or family, you can ask what they've been up to since the last time you saw them
- Current movies and books are always a great conversation starter

During these conversations, avoid controversial topics such as religion and politics. Not only can they kill the festive mood, but they can lead to debate and arguments. The purpose of engaging the audience is to get warmed up. As you talk to more people, you will become more comfortable and build confidence, and eventually, you will enter into a zone where conversation flows naturally. This will all help to prepare you and set the stage for your speech. Not to mention, once you go before the crowd, you'll be less nervous if they're a group of people you've already spoken to. During the speech, you can always look to the people who you held conversations with so that it doesn't feel as awkward. If you pick two or three people in the audience and focus on them, it will feel as though you're having a casual conversation with them, rather than giving a public speech.

Speaking to people before the speech also serves as a positive distraction. It keeps you busy and prevents you from over-thinking about speaking in front of a group of people. This exercise helps to keep your nerves at bay, and carries the added benefit of warming up the audience. They may not know that you're giving a speech yet, but when you get up on stage, they'll think, "Hey, I just spoke to that guy," and they'll be more receptive to what you have to say.

Changing Clothes

Here's a quick note on changing clothes...

In some weddings, there is an opportunity to change clothes between the ceremony and the reception. Many people do this to switch from stuffy formal attire, to more casual clothes they can dance/drink/mingle in. While I do recommend you bring a change of clothes, I would hold off on changing until after your give your speech. Unlike most other guests, you are part of the wedding ceremony and bridal party. People will be taking pictures of you and recording your speech. These memories can last decades and the last thing you want is to remembered for the sweatpants you wore, rather than the speech you gave...

Recording the Speech

Once you've arrived at the venue where you will give the speech, make sure to ask a trusted friend or family member to use your phone to record the speech. This is an important task, so don't pick a teenaged kid, or someone you just met. Avoid picking someone with small children, since kids can sometimes distract them from taking the video.

Now I know what you're saying...

"But, the groom and bride already have a photographer and a video recorder."

Great.

Good for them.

You're still going to have to record with *your* camera.

This is for several reasons:

1. Photos of people are great, but you're about to give the best damn speech they've ever heard, and they'll want a *good* recording as well.

2. Oftentimes, the DJ is in charge of recording the speeches. However, they can become so preoccupied with their other duties that they forget to pay attention to the video recorder, which results in poor quality or no recording at all.

3. Even if there's a person designated to record the wedding, they too cannot be relied on. Sometimes equipment fails, or the video tape just happens to run out just as your speech starts. Yes, you read that correctly, some recorders still use

actual cassettes to record... And this exact problem happened at a wedding where I gave a speech.

4.   As the Father of the Groom, it is not only your duty to give the speech, but also to ensure it is captured for the couple to share for as long as they both shall live.

5.   Worst case scenario, you and the couple have multiple versions and perspectives of the speech to keep as a memento.

6.   Even if the professional photographer/recorder got the whole speech on video, they can take days, weeks, and sometimes even months to give it to the groom and bride. If it's your camera, you can post it to Facebook (or any other social media) almost instantaneously, and all of their friends and family can access it.

Keeping all of those reasons in mind, don't forget to make sure you have enough battery and recording space to capture the speech. The last thing you want is to get an error, or have your camera die as you're giving a speech (yup, this one happened to me too...). If you're using a smartphone, ensure the person recording knows to record horizontally (for the best picture). As silly as it sounds, make sure they know how to unlock the phone as well (especially if you have a code). Lastly, it wouldn't hurt to switch to airplane mode, so that no one can unexpectedly call or text you and interrupt the recording.

Recap:

1. Charge your phone

2. Make sure there is space on the phone to record at least 5-10 minutes
3. Place in airplane mode
4. Designate a trusted friend/family member to record the speech

Execution Phase
The Runway Method: Starting the speech

Just like a plane on a runway, you'll need about a minute or two to gain momentum before taking off into the great unknown. The moments leading up to the speech are what I consider "runway" time, and they are crucial. This is when you will build up the energy that will propel you into the speech. Once it's your turn to speak, stand up straight, and look around at the audience with a smile. Next, walk toward the microphone slowly but deliberately, taking the most direct route possible. Waving at friends and family members is encouraged, as it builds energy and confidence for the speech. Focus on physical energy. When you receive the microphone, shake the person's hand and thank them. If it's the DJ or Father of the Groom, ask the crowd to give them a round of applause. This does two things: 1) it sets the tone for the speech, letting the audience know that you are in charge, and 2) it gives you a moment to collect your thoughts and compose yourself. Once the applause dies down, ask everyone to charge their glasses with a drink to prepare for the toast. Again, you're setting the tone, and settling in.

Establishing Authority

There are key messages that are communigroomed in this "Runway" time. For example, anyone who remembers the novel *Lord of the Flies,* knows that whoever holds the conch is the one in charge. In weddings, the microphone is the symbol of authority. As soon as it is handed to you, the audience sees you as the master of ceremonies.

Providing praise to others is something that leaders and people of authority do. Think back to your childhood. Your parents, teachers, and coaches gave praise. So, when you lead the group in praising the DJ, or Father of the Groom, the same psychological message registers in their minds.

You are in charge.

Giving instruction is yet another characteristic of an authority. Consider your spouse, or boss, or a priest in church. When they give instructions, you comply. This denotes authority. The same holds true when you ask the audience to charge their glasses. They will read this as an instruction, subconsciously preparing them for the very important speech you are about to give.

Establishing Familiarity

Waving to people and shaking hands symbolizes familiarity. Think about politicians or celebrities. They're always waving at crowds and shaking people's hands when approaching a podium. Have you ever asked yourself why they do this? In most cases, they've probably never met anyone in the crowd. The purpose is to send the message that they are a known and trusted entity. Luckily for you, you won't have to fake it. Just wave at a friend or shake someone's hand as you approach the designated speaking area. They will be sure to wave back and smile, because you've just acknowledged them in front of the crowd. This creates familiarity and anticipation with the crowd.

Lastly, early applause equals energy. It gets the audience moving and the blood flowing. The sound of clapping awakens the rest of our senses. This will further prepare everyone for the speech to come. Just before you give the speech, instruct the audience give the groom and bride a hand. You can easily accomplish this by looking toward the couple and saying, "Ladies and gentlemen, don't they look wonderful together? Let's give them a round of applause."

This takes the attention off of you, so that you can calm your nerves and settle into the speech. Moreover, it increases the energy (both physical and emotional--you know there will be some moms out there crying about how beautiful the groom looks) in the room. This will build rapport and familiarity with the audience by acknowledging the main thing you have in common: the groom and bride.

The Fly Zone: The meat of your speech

After completing a minute or two of "Runway" time, you'll be in what I call the "Fly Zone." By this point you should have built up enough momentum, rapport, and energy with the audience that you're ready to "take off" into the speech. No sweat, because you've practiced your speech so many times it's like second nature to you. Nothing can stand in your way.

Right?

Well, sort of...

Let me explain.

Although you've practiced your speech so many times that you could give it in your sleep, there is still one major thing that could get in your way... DISTRACTIONS. During your speech there are a number of things that can throw both you or your audience off balance. Yes, it's sad but true, distractions come in all shapes and sizes, and no one knows exactly where or when they will pop up. Never fear, the Father of the Groom mentor is here! The following is a list of just a few things that are likely to happen during a wedding speech.

Crying babies

Most parents will leave the room if their infant starts to cry. If the noise distracts you or the audience, pause for a moment, collect your thoughts, then start up again by saying, "Now where was I?" If you can, just continue with your speech. If the crying persists and it distracts you, try to make light of the situation with a quick joke. If you acknowledge the child crying, most parents will take that as a cue to remove them from the room.

Children

Kids just love to run a muck during speeches. Some even like to join you at the speaking area (this is especially true if they're your own children). If it's not distracting to your or the audience, just press on. If it is distracting, you have a couple options: 1) Make light of the situation with a joke. Or, 2) have the child join you at the front. When the child approaches, ask them their name and if they're having a good time. Once they answer tell them thanks for the help and ask them to go have a seat with their parents. As they go to their seat, have the audience give the kid a round of applause. Once everyone settles back down, continue your speech where you left off. 3) Ask for a parent to come and get the child.

Crowd Movements

You'd be surprised how many people have to use the bathroom, grab seconds, or get another beer once you start your speech. Many speakers don't anticipate this, so they start to second guess themselves. They worry that their speech isn't captivating enough. Is it so terrible that people aren't even paying attention? No. Don't overthink it. People are hungry and want to grab seconds/desert before anyone else. Just keep talking, you're doing fine.

Wedding Staff

Somehow dishes always seem to break during a speech. If this happens, press on. If the crash was so loud it distracted the audience, pause and allow everyone to collect themselves, then continue with the speech.

Microphone Malfunctions

Unfortunately this happens quite often. Broken mics, missing or dead batteries, and reverbing mics are all common place. If this happens to you, the easiest fix is to turn the microphone off and project your voice to the crowd. While it's not ideal, it's better than tinkering with the device in front of a large group of people.

Blank Stares

Anyone who gives speeches regularly knows that people look really funny when they're listening. If you don't speak to groups often, it may surprise you how many blank stares you see in the crowd. Don't feel discouraged or worried. Unlike one on one conversations, where there is interaction on the other end, large crowds normally go into a completely passive state. This means they'll look as though they're staring right at you, or through you. Don't worry, they're not zombies, nor are they judging you. They're just listening, so keep moving along with your speech.

Photographers

Wedding photographers may record or snap photos of you during the speech. They will try to get angles with you, the groom, the bride, and the audience at any time during your speech. While this isn't a major distractor, it can throw you for a loop if you're not prepared for it. Beyond the official photographer, be prepared to see family members and friends take photos or even come up and kneel in front of you, so they can record the speech.

Outdoor Noises

Sirens, construction, planes, alarms and other background noise are always a threat to outside venues. Ugh! I wish I didn't have to say this, but if you're at an outside reception, your speech will be vulnerable to these types of noises. If it's something temporary like a plane, or police sirens, feel free to pause, until it passes by. However, if it's a car alarm or construction, it's unlikely to stop anytime soon. You'll just have to power through. As mentioned earlier in the book, if you've rehearsed the lines, then you should be at the point where you can give the speech "blindfolded" so to speak.

Emergencies

In the event of an emergency such as a fire alarm, stop the speech immediately and direct everyone to their nearest exit.

I promise that at least one of these distractions will attempt to deter you from accomplishing your speech successfully. More than likely, several of them will happen. However, knowing is half the battle. The ability to adapt to the unexpected is part of what separates the good speakers from the great ones.

EXAMPLE SPEECHES

EXAMPLE 1: Long Toast

BEST SUITED FOR: Extraverts

TIMEFRAME: For those who have several weeks to prepare and practice their speech.

NOTE: The following example is geared toward a father of the groom. However with a few minor adjustments, this can be changed for a grandfather, step father, or a foster father. This is particularly good for people who enjoy speaking in front of people and don't get stage fright.

Spoken words are italicised. Actions are not.

YOUR QUEUE

First, the DJ or MC calls you up to speak.

As you approach, wave at friends or family. If there are other friends or family along the walkway, shake their hands or give high-fives. Once you get to the designated speaking area, ask everyone to charge their glasses, then request applause for the groom and bride.

ADDRESS THE AUDIENCE

Ladies and gentlemen, friends and family, please charge your glasses in preparation for the toast.

(Charge your glass as they charge theirs.)

Welcome everyone.

My name is YOUR NAME And I'm GROOM's father.

It gives me great joy to see so many people here for this momentous occasion. I would like to thank all of the friends and family who have come to share this special day with us. This union couldn't have happened without your support.

TALK ABOUT GROOM

You know, when GROOM was born, we were the happiest parents on earth. I was determined to be the greatest dad ever. I had a dream that someday, GROOM would grow up to be a responsible, and compassionate human being. But, I knew it was our responsibility to guide him down that path.

So we gave him unconditional love and support.

Watching GROOM grow up into the man you see before you was my greatest joy.

ADDRESS GROOM:

GROOM, I stand here today the proudest father that ever lived. You have surpassed all of my expectations and dreams. I want you to know, being your dad has been the greatest privilege of my life.

(Pause for 2-3 seconds)

Ever since you were little, I've always hoped that one day you would find someone to share your life with. Someone to love and cherish. When BRIDE came into your life, I was sure you had met "The One." She is thoughtful, sensitive and loving. I'm so excited that you've found such a dignified woman.

ADDRESS BRIDE

And to you BRIDE, thank you for taking care of my son. If there was one person in this entire world I could pick for him, it would be you. We are blessed to have you as a part of our family.

GIVE ADVICE (Optional)

(Address Couple)

GROOM, BRIDE,

I wish I could tell you that life will be easy from this day forward. But as you know, sometimes obstacles get in the way. All marriages have their fair share of challenges to overcome. When those tough times come, just remember...

We don't just marry a person we can live with.

We marry the person we can't live without.

When you find yourselves entangled difficult situations, don't forget you have someone who will stand by you through thick and thin. Someone that will pick you up when you're down. If you two can hold fast to each other, I'm confident there's no storm you can't weather.

TOAST

(Raise your glass and look to the audience)

Ladies and gentlemen, please join me in a toast.

GROOM and BRIDE,

May you be blessed with joy and happiness all the days of your lives.

Take a sip of your drink, then place it on the table. Everyone will start applauding. Clap with the audience and gesture toward the groom and bride. Usually, the photographer will ask you to pose with the wedding couple for a picture. Either way, be sure to hand the microphone back to the DJ before you head back to your seat. Again, feel free to wave, hug, or shake hands on the way back to your seat.

EXAMPLE 2: Medium Toast

BEST SUITED FOR: Extraverts/Introverts

TIMEFRAME: For those who have 5-10 days to prepare and practice their speech.

NOTE: The following example is geared toward a father of the groom. However with a few minor adjustments, this can be changed for a grandfather, step father, or a foster father. This particular speech can accommodate both introverts and extraverts in the sense that it is not too long, nor too short. The words are simple yet powerful. While this does not require as much preparation as the example one, I still recommend at least 5-10 days of practice.

Spoken words are italicised. Actions are not.

YOUR QUEUE

First, the DJ or MC calls you up to speak.

As you approach, wave at friends or family. If there are other friends or family along the walkway, shake their hands or give high-fives. Once you get to the designated speaking area, ask everyone to charge their glasses, then request applause for the groom and bride.

ADDRESS THE AUDIENCE

Ladies and gentlemen, friends and family, please charge your glasses in preparation for the toast.

(Charge your glass as they charge theirs.)

Welcome everyone.

My name is YOUR NAME And I'm GROOM's father.

It brings me great joy to see so many people here for this moment. I would like to thank all of the friends and family who have come to share this special day with us. This couldn't have happened without your support.

ADDRESS GROOM:

GROOM, I stand here today the proudest father that ever lived. You have surpassed all of my expectations. I want you to know, being your dad has been the greatest privilege of my life.

Ever since you were little, I've always hoped that one day you would find someone to share your life with. Someone to love and cherish. When BRIDE came into your life, I was sure you met "The One." She is thoughtful, sensitive and loving.

ADDRESS BRIDE

BRIDE, thank you for taking care of my son. If there was one person in this entire world I could pick for him, it would be you. We are blessed to have you.

TOAST

(Raise your glass and look to the audience)

Ladies and gentlemen, please join me in a toast.

GROOM and BRIDE,

May you be blessed with joy and happiness all the days of your lives.

Take a sip of your drink, then place it on the table. Everyone will start applauding. Clap with the audience and gesture toward the groom and bride. Usually, the photographer will ask you to pose with the wedding couple for a picture. Either way, be sure to hand the microphone back to the DJ before you head back to your seat. Again, feel free to wave, hug, or shake hands on the way back to your seat.

EXAMPLE 3: Short Toast

BEST SUITED FOR: Introverts
TIMEFRAME: For those who have less than five days to prepare and practice their speech.
NOTE: The following example is geared toward a father of the groom. However with a few minor adjustments, this can be changed for a grandfather, step father, or a foster father. This particular speech is geared for introverts. However it can also help those who have less than five days to prepare a speech.

Spoken words are italicised. Actions are not.

YOUR QUEUE

First, the DJ or MC calls you up to speak.

As you approach, wave at friends or family. If there are other friends or family along the walkway, shake their hands or give high-fives. Once you get to the designated speaking area, ask everyone to charge their glasses, then request applause for the groom and bride.

ADDRESS THE AUDIENCE

Ladies and gentlemen, friends and family, please charge your glasses in preparation for the toast.

(Charge your glass as they charge theirs.)

Welcome everyone.

My name is YOUR NAME And I'm GROOM's father.

I'm not one for long speeches, so I'll keep it short.

Today two lives became one and today I am the proudest father that ever lived.

TOAST

(Raise your glass and look to the audience)
Ladies and gentlemen, please join me in a toast.
GROOM and BRIDE,
May you be blessed with joy and happiness all the days of your lives.

Take a sip of your drink, then place it on the table. Everyone will start applauding. Clap with the audience and gesture toward the groom and bride. Usually, the photographer will ask you to pose with the wedding couple for a picture. Either way, be sure to hand the microphone back to the DJ before you head back to your seat. Again, feel free to wave, hug, or shake hands on the way back to your seat.

EXAMPLE 4: The Quickest and Easiest Toast

BEST SUITED FOR: Introverts or eeople with no time to prepare
TIMEFRAME: This literally takes five minutes to learn
NOTE: The following example is geared toward a father of the groom. However with a few minor adjustments, this can be changed for a grandfather, step father, or a foster father. This particular speech is geared for introverts. However it can also help those who no time to prepar their speech.

Spoken words are italicised. Actions are not.

YOUR QUEUE

First, the DJ or MC calls you up to speak.

As you approach, wave at friends or family. If there are other friends or family along the walkway, shake their hands or give high-fives. Once you get to the designated speaking area, ask everyone to charge their glasses, then request applause for the groom and bride.

TOAST

(Raise your glass and look to the audience)
Ladies and gentlemen, please join me in a toast.
GROOM and BRIDE,
May you be blessed with joy and happiness all the days of your lives.

Take a sip of your drink, then place it on the table. Everyone will start applauding. Clap with the audience and gesture toward the groom and bride. Usually, the photographer will ask you to pose with the wedding couple for a picture. Either way, be sure to hand the microphone back to the DJ before you head back to your seat. Again, feel free to wave, hug, or shake hands on the way back to your seat.

CONCLUSION

Hopefully by this point, you're well on your way to creating a killer speech. You should have a general idea of what your responsibilities are as the Father of the Groom and some of the key points of the talk. Don't forget to prepare yourself by creating an outline and practicing as much as possible. Also follow the program to the T. The more you rehearse the speech, the better it will become, and the easier it will be to perform. This will allow you to speak with confidence on the big day. Feel free to tweak the speech toward your strengths. If you're more of an introvert, try to keep the speech as short as possible. If you're an extravert, don't push past ten minutes. If you take the steps detailed in this book, you'll give a speech that will awe audience members, and leave the groom and bride happy with their decision. Ultimately, we hope this book helps you carry out your duties as the Father of the Groom, and allows you to give the best speech you possibly can.

Now, go out there and break a leg!

Thank You From Story Ninjas

Story Ninjas Publishing would like to thank you for reading our book. We hope you found value in this product and would love to hear your feedback. Please provide your constructive criticism in a review on Amazon. Also feel free to share this book through the various social media platforms.

About Story Ninjas

Story Ninjas Publishing is an independent book publisher. Our stories range from science fiction to paranormal romance. Our goal is to create stories that are not only entertaining, but endearing. We believe engaging narrative can lead to personal growth. Through unforgettable characters and powerful plot we portray themes that are relevant for today's issues.

You can find more Story Ninja's products here.

Follow Story Ninjas!!!
Twitter: @StoryNinjas
Youtube: @StoryNinjas
Amazon: Story Ninjas

G+: +Story Ninjas
Facebook: StoryNinjasHQ
LinkedIn: Story-Ninjas
Blogger: Story-NinjasHQ

Printed in Great Britain
by Amazon

79978728R00031